Mel Brooks

A Little Golden Book® Biography

To my grand gigglers: N, D, V, and the two M's —C.M.

By Christy Mihaly
Illustrated by Kelly Kennedy

 A GOLDEN BOOK • NEW YORK

Text copyright © 2024 by Christy Mihaly
Cover art and interior illustrations copyright © 2024 by Kelly Kennedy
All rights reserved. Published in the United States by Golden Books, an imprint of
Random House Children's Books, a division of Penguin Random House LLC, 1745 Broadway,
New York, NY 10019. Golden Books, A Golden Book, A Little Golden Book, the G colophon,
and the distinctive gold spine are registered trademarks of Penguin Random House LLC.
rhcbooks.com
Educators and librarians, for a variety of teaching tools, visit us at RHTeachersLibrarians.com
Library of Congress Control Number: 2022950274
ISBN 978-0-593-64839-1 (trade) — ISBN 978-0-593-64840-7 (ebook)
Printed in the United States of America
10 9 8 7 6 5 4 3 2 1

On June 28, 1926, Max and Kate Kaminsky welcomed their fourth son, Melvin, into the world. Their Brooklyn, New York, neighborhood was crowded with Jewish immigrants. Their apartment was crowded with boys.

When Melvin was two, his father died, but as the boys grew up, their mother, aunts, uncles, and grandparents surrounded them with love and laughter. The four boys shared one bedroom, but Melvin didn't mind—his brothers kept him warm.

Melvin and his pals played stickball and rode homemade scooters. Melvin wasn't the best athlete, but he told the funniest stories. He did silly stunts and imitations. He loved being the center of attention.

One day, Uncle Joe received free tickets to *Anything Goes*, a Broadway musical. He took nine-year-old Melvin to the show. Wow! The dancing and singing were dazzling. Melvin laughed and laughed and applauded until his hands hurt. That's when he knew he wanted to be in show business.

In high school, Melvin got a drum set—and a stage name. He thought his mother's family name, Brookman, sounded better than Kaminsky for a performer. But since it was too long to fit on his drum, he became "Mel Brooks."

At fourteen, Mel got a summer job. It was at a resort in the Catskill Mountains, popular with Jewish New Yorkers. The resort offered nightly entertainment. Mel washed dishes, cleared tables, and hoped for a lucky break.

When an actor sprained his ankle and couldn't perform one night, guess who was called in to replace him.

It was Mel's stage debut! As the curtain rose, his hands shook. The script called for him to pour a glass of water. But Mel was so nervous he dropped the glass. *Crash!*

In the stunned silence, Mel walked to the edge of the stage. He pulled off his character's wig and cried, "I'm only fourteen! I've never done this before!" The audience roared with laughter.

Mel loved getting laughs. He worked several summers in the Catskills, amusing guests by making silly faces and telling jokes. He learned which jokes worked—and which were duds.

When the United States entered World War II, Mel's brothers signed up to fight. Mel didn't like war, but he wanted to help, too. So he joined the army when he turned eighteen.

Mel was stationed in Europe when the war ended. During his last months there, he worked with the army's Special Services to provide entertainment for the troops.

Back home after the war, Mel struggled to find work in show business. Then funnyman Sid Caesar hired Mel to write jokes for him.

In 1950, Sid began starring in a new television variety show called *Your Show of Shows.* Mel worked with a team of writers, churning out jokes and skits for the show each week. One writer, Carl Reiner, became Mel's best friend.

During this time, Mel met Florence Baum, a Broadway dancer. They married and had three children, Stephanie, Nicky, and Eddie.

Later on, Mel married his second wife, Anne Bancroft. She was a talented and successful actress. They had a son, Max, and a very long and happy marriage.

Mel worked with Sid on different shows for almost ten years. Then Sid's last show was canceled, and Mel was out of a job. It was a hard time, but his friends, especially Carl Reiner, kept him laughing.

Carl and Mel developed a comedy routine they called "The 2000 Year Old Man." They performed it for friends at parties. Mel pretended to be two thousand years old. Carl asked him questions. Mel gave funny answers about his hundreds of wives and thousands of children, using his grandfather's Yiddish accent.

In 1960, Carl and Mel made a recording of their routine. The record was a hit! It made them famous.

Mel continued to do writing projects but earned hardly any money. He needed to find regular work.

Finally, he was hired to help create a new TV series. The result was *Get Smart*, a comedy about a bumbling secret agent. Mel said agent Maxwell Smart should communicate with a secret "shoe phone." (Cell phones hadn't been invented yet!) The series was a big success.

Then Mel wanted to write a funny movie. The script needed two songs. Mel was not a songwriter, but Anne believed he could do anything. With his wife's encouragement, he wrote the songs.

Mel's movie, *The Producers,* was released in 1967. Some critics said the comedy was awful. But Mel got the last laugh and won the Academy Award for Best Original Screenplay.

Not many people went to see *The Producers* or Mel's next movie, *The Twelve Chairs*, either. But he kept writing.

In 1974, Mel released *Young Frankenstein*. Considered among the funniest movies ever, *Young Frankenstein* made fun of classic horror films. Audiences laughed and cheered—and looked forward to whatever Mel did next.

Mel made more than forty movies. He acted in many of them. In 1983, Mel and Anne costarred in the movie *To Be or Not to Be*. They made a great team!

Thirty years after writing *The Producers*, Mel turned the movie into a musical play. He almost hired a "real" Broadway songwriter, but Anne said he could write the songs. And he did.

In 2001, *The Producers* became Broadway's biggest show. It won twelve Tony Awards—an all-time record! Mel had come a long way since falling in love with Broadway as a boy.

Later in life, Mel had a new favorite role: being a grandpa. And he worked as a voice actor for cartoon characters. He liked knowing his grandchildren would hear his voice in animated movies. In *Toy Story 4*, Mel and Carl had fun recording the voices of Melephant Brooks and Carl Reineroceros.

At age ninety, Mel received the National Medal of Arts in honor of his "lifetime of making the world laugh." President Barack Obama hung a large gold medal around Mel's neck.

Mel pretended to fall over because the medal was so heavy. Everyone laughed.

As usual, he loved hearing the explosion of laughter!